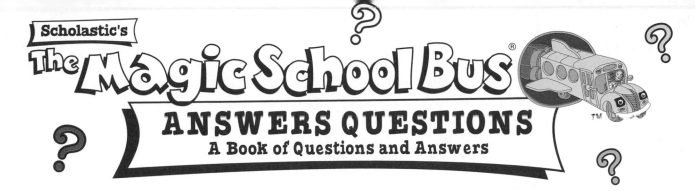

SCHOLASTIC INC.
New York Toronto London Auckland Sydney

From the animated series
produced by Scholastic Entertainment, Inc.
Based on *The Magic School Bus* books
written by Joanna Cole and illustrated by Bruce Degen.

TV tie-in adaptation by Anne Schreiber.

ISBN 0-439-04332-8

12 11 10 9 8 7 6 5 4 3 2 1   9/9 0 1 2 3 4/0

Printed in the U.S.A.   23
First Scholastic Trade paperback printing, February 1999

A STICKY QUESTION
How did we get into this mess?

By going on a field trip on the Magic School Bus.
Come along and make mistakes, get messy, and
ASK QUESTIONS!

There's no such thing
as a silly question.

Except in this book.

Why are they after us?

It's not us they're after, it's the heat lamp.

How do cold-blooded animals stay warm?

Cold-blooded animals need to move to warm places to warm up and cool places to cool down. All reptiles are cold-blooded. Snakes, turtles and lizards are reptiles. Frogs are also cold-blooded. But they're amphibians. Insects and fish are cold-blooded too.

Can you name some warm-blooded animals?
(Turn to page 28 for the answer.)

4

Do people and lizards cool down the same way?

No. People can shiver to warm up and sweat to cool down. But lizards can't shiver or sweat. Instead, they have to move from place to place to keep their bodies comfortable.

SOUND QUESTIONS

Do sounds have good vibrations?

Without vibrations, or movements, there would be no sounds. As overnight guests at the sound museum, Ms. Frizzle's class learned that sound vibrations travel in waves that your eyes cannot see but your ears can hear. Fast vibrations make high sounds. Slow vibrations make low sounds.

What's an echo? echo? echo?

An echo is caused by a sound that hits something — like a wall or a mountain. When the sound waves hit the hard surface, they bounce back and we hear the sound again. In a tunnel, the sound waves may bounce around many times and we hear the sound again and again, again, gain, gn, gn. . . .

What do you think happens to sounds that do not hit a surface and bounce back?
(Turn to page 28 for the answer.)

What is a force?

A force is a force, of course, of course. And that means a push
or a pull. Forces are everywhere. Here are some forceful examples:
Swinging on a swing, hitting a hockey puck with a stick, punching
a volleyball, pulling a wagon up a hill, speeding down a hill on a
bicycle, and, of course, swinging a baseball bat. And that's just
the beginning.

What is friction? Why do I need it?

Friction is a force that slows down or stops things from moving. You may not be able to see friction, but you can feel it. A patch of dirt poking through the snow slows down your sled. The brakes of your bike press on the wheel to stop it. Friction is all around. If there were no friction, there'd be no way to stop moving objects like sliding bodies, flying balls, or running feet.

Where can you be almost frictionless?
(Turn to page 28 for the answer.)

9

FISHY QUESTIONS

Why don't these salmon just go with the flow?

These salmon are not going with the flow. In fact, they're going against it! They started their journey in the ocean. Now they're swimming upstream through a freshwater river. Where are they headed? To the place they were born. What will they do there? Lay their eggs.

Where do you think the baby salmon will go after they hatch? (Turn to page 28 for the answer.)

How do salmon find their way home?

Salmon remember where they were born. From far away, they smell something that reminds them of their first home. They swim toward the smell. As home gets closer, the smell grows stronger. Ah, the sweet smell of home. It's just common scents!

HOT QUESTIONS

How do animals survive in the desert?

The desert may be tough, but it's home sweet home to many animals including lizards, tortoises, jackrabbits, owls, scorpions, and even foxes. How do these animals live with little water, little shelter, and the hot, hot days and cold, cold nights? Adaptations!

Adaptations are the special behaviors or body parts that animals have to keep them comfortable in their homes.

Desert animals have spiny or tough bodies to protect them from predators, they stay under cover during the hot days, and they each have special adaptations to stay cool and wet.

What's so hot about these desert animals?

The desert tortoise is very well adapted to its desert home. It digs under the sand and sleeps through the desert summer.

The kangaroo rat is another animal with a special adaptation. It can go its whole life without ever drinking water. It gets all the water it needs from its food.

Can you think of a desert plant with a special adaptation?

(Turn to page 28 for the answer.)

13

QUESTIONS ABOUT HOME

Who lives in this pond habitat?

An animal's habitat is its home. Animals use their habitats to find food and stay safe from predators.

This dragonfly's great-, great-, great-, great-grandfather lived in the time of the dinosaurs. Back then, one kind of dragonfly had a wingspan as wide as a small truck.

This frog needs insects to eat, water to drink, and a safe place to lay her eggs. Frogs use their sticky tongues to catch bugs.

These beavers are into home improvement. By building a dam, they can turn a fast-moving stream into a pond. Their lodge is very comfy, but good luck finding the door — it's underwater!

A great blue heron lives high up in the trees. It uses its long beak to hunt fish, insects, mice, and even frogs. Herons can stand four feet tall — that's about as tall as a first-grader!

Watch out, Wanda!

Stop!

EARTHY QUESTIONS

Why do bees need flowers?

Bees like it sweet. So they suck the sweet nectar out of flowers. Now that's interesting bee-havior!

Why do flowers need bees?

When a bee drinks nectar from a flower, pollen sticks to its body.
When the bee moves to the next flower, it drops off the pollen
from the first flower. Then that flower can use the new pollen to
grow seeds. More pollen, more seeds. More seeds, more flowers.

How do you think flowers attract bees?
(Turn to page 29 for the answer.)

DELICIOUS QUESTIONS

What does baking have to do with chemistry?

Can you think of a chemical reaction that you can eat when you go camping?
(Turn to page 29 for the answer.)

18

Chemistry is mixing things together to make something new. The kids in Ms. Frizzle's class learned that the ingredients they used to bake a cake were made up of smaller parts. By mixing the ingredients together, the small parts from one ingredient teamed up with the small parts from another ingredient and something new was formed. Add heat to bread and you get toast. Add air to cream and you get butter. Is it cooking or is it chemistry? It's both!

What do salt and sugar look like up close and personal?

Sugar and salt are real jewels — microscopically speaking, of course. Up close, sugar is made of tiny crystals that look like diamonds. Salt looks like rectangular towers or tiny saltscrapers.

Who cares about plants?

I liked it better when we were on the top of the food chain.

You should! If there were no plants, there'd be no you. Phytoplankton, or tiny ocean plants, are eaten by zooplankton, which are eaten by little fish, which are eaten by bigger fish, which are eaten by . . . you. (Or bears, if they get there first.) That's called a food chain, and plants are always at the bottom. Who's on top? You!

Can you think of a land food chain that you are also a part of? (Turn to page 29 for the answer.)

What do plants eat?

Plants don't eat the same way animals do, but they do need energy to live. And they get that energy directly from the sun. Now that's a bright idea!

FLIGHTY QUESTIONS

What keeps this plane in the air?

Hop on board the Magic School Plane with Wildcat Wanda at the controls. There you'll find out that air, moving across the wings of a plane, holds the plane up in the sky. Slow or stop the moving air, and oops, down goes the plane. Moving air makes the plane stay in the sky. That's called lift. No lift — bye, bye sky!

If propellers are so important, why don't birds have them?

An airplane uses its propeller to pull it forward. This forward motion keeps air moving across its wings so the plane stays in the air. A bird has to keep its body moving forward, too. But birds have built in propellers — wings! A bird moves its body forward with special wing feathers or by flapping its wings up and down while it flies.

How do you think a bird's tail and a plane's tail are alike? (Turn to page 29 for the answer.)

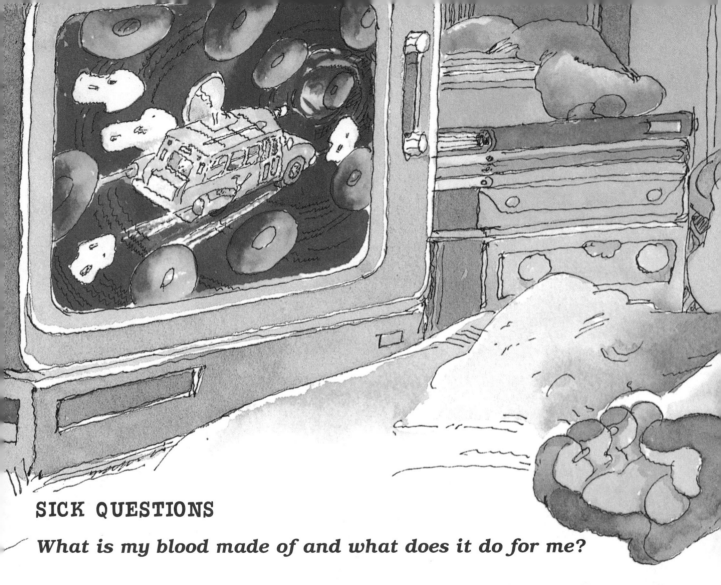

SICK QUESTIONS

What is my blood made of and what does it do for me?

Ms. Frizzle and her class have seen more of Ralphie than they wanted. When they traveled through Ralphie's bloodstream, they noticed that his blood was made of a clear liquid with red and white parts floating inside. Those were Ralphie's red and white blood cells. His red blood cells carried oxygen all over his body. His white blood cells found and killed the germs that were making him sick.

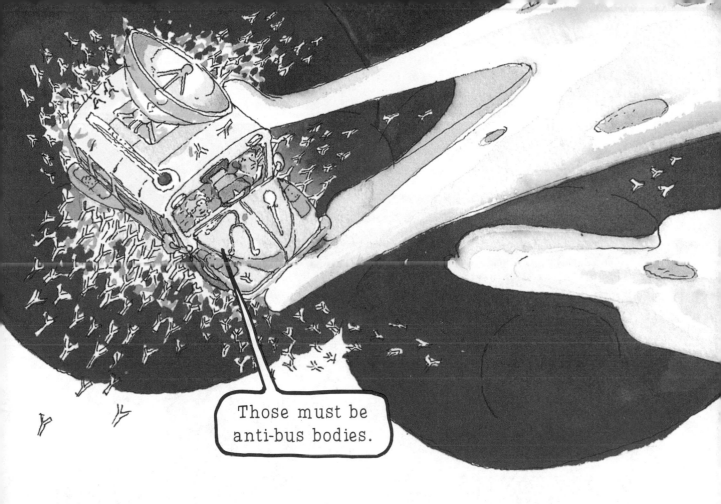

How does my body keep me healthy?

Your body works hard to keep you well. Your skin protects you from germs. And if a germ does happen to get inside, watch out! Your white blood cells send out scouts called antibodies. They mark the germs and bam! The battle is on!

What can you do to help your body stay healthy?
(Turn to page 29 for the answer.)

BUTTERFLY QUESTIONS

How do butterflies protect themselves?

Butterflies are full of surprises. Many butterflies and moths have dull colors that blend into their habitats. Butterflies can look like weeds, leaves, or even tree bark. Can you find the butterfly in this picture?

Is this scary animal a bog beast?

No way! This animal may look scary, but it's really just a colorful butterfly in disguise. Some butterflies are brightly colored or have markings that look like bulging eyes. This makes them look fierce and keeps them from becoming breakfast for a bird.

YOU ASKED THE QUESTIONS.
NOW FIND THE ANSWERS.

Page 4:

Can you name some warm-blooded animals?

Dog, person, owl, hippo . . . any mammal or bird is correct.

Page 7:

What do you think happens to sounds that do not hit a surface and bounce back?

They will keep going on and on and grow weaker as they mix with other sound waves.

Page 9:

Where can you be almost frictionless?

On ice, on a slide, on any slippery surface.

Page 10:

Where do you think the baby salmon will go after they hatch?

When they grow up, they will go to the ocean and later migrate back to the freshwater river where they were born.

Page 13:

Can you think of a desert plant with a special adaptation?

Answers can include plants with spiny leaves like cactus, or with thick, leathery leaves like yucca or aloe.

Page 17:

How do you think flowers attract bees?
With bright colors, sweet smells, and tubes that lead to the nectar.

Page 18:

Can you think of a chemical reaction that you can eat when you go camping?
S'mores, popcorn, toasted marshmallows

Page 20:

Can you think of a land food chain that you are also a part of?
Answers will vary but should all begin with plants such as grass or grains. For example, grass is eaten by cows, and cows are eaten by people.

Page 23:

How do you think a bird's tail and a plane's tail are alike?
Both are used for steering and keeping steady.

Page 25:

What can you do to help your body stay healthy?
Eat healthy foods, wash your hands, rest, exercise.

GET MESSY! TAKE THE TEST.

Page 3: *How does a spider keep from getting caught in its own web?*
1. It wears a special no-stick suit.
2. It stays away from the sticky threads.
3. It never goes back to the same web twice.

Pages 4-5: *Which of these animals is cold-blooded?*
1. a dolphin
2. a snake
3. a human

Pages 6-7: *True or False?*
Low sounds are caused by vibrations that travel very low to the ground.

Pages 8-9: *Which material has the least friction?*
1. carpeting
2. sand
3. ice

Pages 10-11: *Why do salmon swim upstream?*
1. for exercise
2. to lay their eggs
3. to hide from fishermen

Pages 12-13: *True or False?*
Many desert animals hunt during the hot day so they can sleep at night when it's too cold to hunt.

Pages 14-15: *True or False?*
Beavers can create a habitat by turning a running stream into a quiet pond.

Pages 16-17: *Which part of a flower do bees eat?*
1. the nectar
2. the petals
3. the seeds

Pages 18-19: *Which one is not a chemical reaction?*
1. heating bread to make toast
2. mixing flour, butter, and eggs to make cake
3. mixing cornflakes and raisins

Pages 20-21: *Where do most plants get their energy from?*
1. They eat smaller plants.
2. They eat small insects.
3. the sun

Pages 22-23: *What would happen to a plane if air stopped moving across its wings?*
1. It would fall to the ground.
2. It would turn to the left.
3. It would keep going.

Pages 24-25: *True or False?*
There are things floating in your blood right now.

Pages 26-27: *True or False?*
Some butterflies protect themselves by pretending to have big, bulging eyes.

(Turn to page 32 for the answers.)

THE ANSWERS!

Page 3: 2. It stays away from the sticky threads.

Pages 4-5: 2. a snake

Pages 6-7: False

Pages 8-9: 3. ice

Pages 10-11: 2. to lay their eggs

Pages 12-13: False

Pages 14-15: True

Pages 16-17: 1. the nectar

Pages 18-19: 3. mixing cornflakes and raisins

Pages 20-21: 3. the sun

Pages 22-23: 1. It would fall to the ground.

Pages 24-25: True

Pages 26-27: True

As I always say, a good answer deserves a good question.